BRITAIN IN OLD PHOTOGRAPHS

STRATFORD,
WEST HAM & THE
ROYAL DOCKS

STEPHEN PEWSEY

SUTTON PUBLISHING LIMITED

Sutton Publishing Limited
Phoenix Mill · Thrupp · Stroud
Gloucestershire · GL5 2BU

First published 1996

Cover photographs: *front*: The inauguration
ceremony of West Ham Tramways electric tram
service, 27 February 1904; *back*: A crowd
gathered outside the Stratford Wireless Shop
hoping to hear the latest news via the then
newfangled wireless, Stratford High Street,
1926.

British Library Cataloguing in Publication Data
A catalogue record for this book is available from the
British Library.

ISBN 0-7509-1417-3

Typeset in 10/12 Perpetua.
Typesetting and origination by
Sutton Publishing Limited.
Printed in Great Britain by
Ebenezer Baylis, Worcester.

CONTENTS

Beckton Road, Canning Town, c. 1890. This scene typifies the terraced housing erected in the south of the borough in the late nineteenth century, much of it jerry-built and without connections to mains drainage and water. In this scene building work is still in hand (note the bricks and timber) while tenants look on. The details of the door and window mouldings and brickwork indicate that these were rather better quality houses than others in the area.

INTRODUCTION

Stratford and West Ham are gateway districts between Essex and London. Originally a rural parish, West Ham lies on the east bank of the River Lea and so before the growth of London it was the last place in Essex before London and the first staging post in Essex from London. This proximity to London was the key to West Ham's growth. The great Roman road between London and Colchester was diverted through Stratford in the twelfth century when Bow Bridge was built.

The subsequent development of Stratford – the largest settlement in West Ham – was based on bread and cattle. Corn from Essex was brought to the many windmills and water-mills along the Lea and its back rivers. Flour from the corn was turned into bread using ovens fired with wood from Epping Forest, which then stretched down almost to the Romford Road. Stratford bakers were exempt from City guild controls and were frequently in court for giving short measure. Cattle were brought to Stratford from the eastern counties for slaughter or onward transit to London, and tanning and other leather-based industries developed there. The presence of a large monastic foundation with many royal connections, Stratford Langthorne Abbey, no doubt attracted further wealth to the area.

The River Lea was the stimulus for further early industrial activity. Silk-weaving and calico-printing were undertaken in the seventeenth and eighteenth centuries and Bow porcelain was made in Stratford in the mid-eighteenth century. Distilling and gunpowder-making were also important. Daniel Defoe noted the rapid growth of Stratford in 1722.

The rest of the parish comprised a scattering of small agricultural hamlets which included Plaistow, Church Lane, Forest Gate and Upton. The marshland in the south of the parish was used for grazing cattle and pasturing horses. Places like Upton and Plaistow were pleasant enough rural retreats to attract City merchants, who built substantial houses there.

However, the inexorable growth of London had a profound effect on the whole area, particularly after 1844 when the Metropolitan Building Act severely restricted many toxic and noxious industries from operating in London and Middlesex. The result of this was that many of these industries relocated across the Essex border to Stratford and West Ham. The banks of the Lea, and soon the Thames as well, quickly became lined with factories rendering down animal carcasses for tallow, soap and glue, chemical plants producing acids, pharmaceuticals, printing inks and a vast range of other products too poisonous to manufacture nearer the capital.

The railway arrived at about the same time and, together with the development of the Royal Group of Docks from 1855, spurred on a further massive growth of West Ham's industrial capability. The dreary Thames-side marshes were transformed into a huge manufacturing and engineering complex which rivalled the great northern cities and, in industry's wake, housing sprang up with dizzying rapidity. Many of the new terraces were jerry-built with no connections to mains water or sewage supply, and infectious disease rampaged freely for some years. Despite the many factories, work was not always easy to come by and for the thousands flocking into Stratford and West Ham, poverty and harsh living conditions were often the only reward for their search for a better life. Out of the hardship an enduring spirit emerged which has come to characterize the Westhammer, a gritty down-to-earth attitude with close bonds between neighbours and families based on mutual support through shared trials and a quick sense of humour.

By the late nineteenth century the separate hamlets of Plaistow, Stratford, Upton, Canning Town and Forest Gate had merged in a sea of bricks and mortar and West Ham was the eighth largest town in Britain. The story of Victorian and early twentieth-century Stratford and West Ham was one of a struggle to cope with the social consequences of this immense population crammed into a small area. The district was the cradle of the modern trade union movement and socialism, with progressive politics always important on West Ham Council. West Ham became a municipal borough in 1886 and a county borough only three years later.

The town's population peaked at 300,860 in 1921, but the Blitz changed the face of West Ham for ever. Mass evacuation in 1940 followed devastating bombing, with V-1 and V-2 attacks in 1944–5 which all combined to destroy and depopulate large parts of the borough. Major rebuilding followed in the postwar years and the area underwent many changes. Familiar landmarks disappeared and the area became far more cosmopolitan as new residents moved in, particularly from the Caribbean and south Asia. In 1965 West Ham and its neighbour East Ham were amalgamated to form the London Borough of Newham, thus ending a thousand-year link with Essex. Industry has declined sharply in recent years and the Royal Docks have closed.

There is much that is still changing, however. There has been some redevelopment in Dockland and Stratford has benefited from becoming a City Challenge zone, with much infrastructure work taking place to restore transport and social facilities and to bring jobs back to the area. Stratford in particular seems destined to recover its historic position as a regional transport interchange, with the Docklands Light Railway and Jubilee Line converging on the town centre. There is also the likelihood of a Channel Tunnel station being built, most fittingly, on the site of the old Great Eastern works to take Stratford and West Ham into the twenty-first century.

EARLY HISTORY

Bow Bridge. First built in about 1100 by Queen Maud (wife of Henry I) reputedly after she fell in the River Lea at the ford (Old Ford) on the old Roman road out of London. It was one of the first arched stone bridges built in England since the Roman occupation, hence the 'bow' name; for its time it was a technological wonder. It was also the scene of a skirmish in 1648 during the Civil War. This engraving dates from just before the demolition of the original bridge in 1835. It was rebuilt again in 1906 and was superseded by a concrete flyover in the 1960s.

Stratford Langthorne Abbey. Founded in 1135 by·William de Monfichet, Stratford Langthorne became one of the richest and most important Cistercian establishments in England. Visited by both Henry II and Henry III, it was sacked during the Peasants' Revolt of 1381. The abbey was dissolved in 1538. This engraving shows the 'Great Gate' in 1764, which survived until about 1825. The whole monastic complex now lies beneath the Docklands Light Railway and the Jubilee Line.

Abbey fragments. Many parts of the abbey survived the Dissolution, though in an increasingly fragmentary condition through the passage of time. This thirteenth-century arch survived until about 1870 in the wall of the Adam and Eve pub.

The River Lea. The Lea and its complex network of back rivers have historically formed both a barrier and a gateway between Essex and London. Stratford developed through the Middle Ages as a trading centre, particularly for cattle – for which Essex was famous – and baking. Essex corn was ground in the many mills along the Lea (both water-mills and windmills) and baked in ovens fuelled with faggots from nearby Epping Forest; this early industrial process supplied much of the beef and bread London required.

Abbey Mills, 1832. There were eight water-mills along the Lea in 1086. Abbey Mill on the Channelsea was one such mill, this particular building dating from the seventeenth century. It burnt down on 30 April 1862.

Windmill at West Ham. This watercolour shows an unknown mill, but it is probably St Thomas or Pudding Mill, also known as Stent's Mill. It had disappeared by the mid-nineteenth century. The intricate network of back rivers of the Lea at Stratford was once claimed as the work of King Alfred as part of his siege of Danish marauders in the ninth century, but it was probably dug in the tenth or eleventh century specifically to provide water-power for mills.

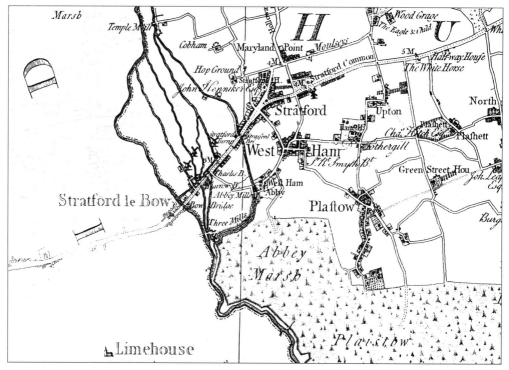

Chapman & André's map of 1777. These two cartographers prepared the first accurate large-scale map of Essex, at a scale of 2 inches to the mile, enough to show individual buildings. This section shows the parish of West Ham. The southern half of the parish was the marshland of Plaistow Level used for cattle grazing. In the north there were three settlements; Stratford, along Stratford High Street; West Ham, clustered round the parish church; and Plaistow, around its village green. Other hamlets included Upton and Maryland Point.

SECTION TWO

CHURCHES

West Ham parish church. Dedicated to All Saints, the parish church was built in about 1180 and has undergone many alterations since. It was enlarged in the thirteenth century and the fine tower added in the fifteenth century; the broad aisles were added in the sixteenth century. As West Ham grew from village to industrial conurbation in the Victorian era, the church was heavily restored. Sir Charles Gilbert Scott (the architect of the Albert Memorial) designed the ornate reredos. Many fine monuments survive in the church, including those to Sir Thomas Foot, Cromwellian Lord Mayor of London and Sir Thomas Smyth, Restoration Lord Mayor.

St John's Church, Stratford. This view shows a snowy scene, *c.* 1886. Built in 1834 as a chapel-of-ease for booming Stratford, the church is now a town centre landmark, with its mellow yellow brick and striking spire. The dome of the town hall can be seen beyond. The Martyrs' Memorial (not seen here) stands in front of the church commemorating thirteen Protestants burnt at the stake on Stratford Green in 1556 (see p.41)

St Mary's Church, Plaistow. Like Stratford, this rapidly-growing district also became a parish in its own right in the early Victorian period. There have been three churches on this site, the first built in an ornate style in 1830. As a result of the campaigning social work and financial appeals of the dynamic vicar Thomas Given-Wilson, the church was rebuilt in 1894 on a grand scale, as seen in this view.

Another view of St Mary's Church, Plaistow. This monument to evangelical Christianity was demolished in 1977 and rebuilt on a much smaller scale and in a modern architectural idiom in 1981.

Emmanuel Church, Forest Gate, *c.* 1927. This plain, but handsome, church opened in 1852 on Romford Road. The north aisle was enlarged to form a distinctive double nave in 1890.

St Luke, Victoria Docks, *c.* 1905. Built in 1875, the church, known as the 'Cathedral of Canning Town', was badly damaged in the Blitz, but later restored. The Boyd Working Men's Institute can be seen on the right of the church. The church was converted for community use in 1996.

Woodgrange Baptist Church, Romford Road, *c.* 1905. West Ham was always a bastion of nonconformity with a vast range of Protestant denominations in the nineteenth century and chapels springing up on every corner. The Baptists were one of the earliest of the Protestant denominations, being recorded as early as 1676. Woodgrange Baptist Church, built in 1882, was enlarged in 1901 and was easily the largest Baptist church in West Ham.

Holy Trinity Church, Canning Town. The slender spire of Holy Trinity soars above the humble roofs of Canning Town in this drawing. Opened in 1867, Holy Trinity stood on the corner of Hermit Road. It suffered during the war and was closed in 1948 before being demolished and the site covered with flats.

Stratford Methodist Church, The Grove, *c.* 1908. Note the grand columns of this classically styled Methodist church, built in 1871. The church was demolished in 1953. The spire of Stratford Congregational Church can be seen opposite. Both Congregationalism and Methodism were important forces for social action in West Ham, supporting much voluntary work and helping create a climate for social action. John Wesley himself, founder of Methodism, had visited West Ham in 1739.

Brickfields Congregational Church, *c.* 1936. This church was founded as early as 1662 and the building shown here dates from the year of the American Revolution, 1776.

Stratford Congregational Church, *c.* 1900. The spire towers over the terrace below. The church was built on a grand scale in 1866–7 and known as 'Settles Folly' after the man who financed its construction. Closed in 1941 and later used as a furniture factory, the church burnt down in 1953.

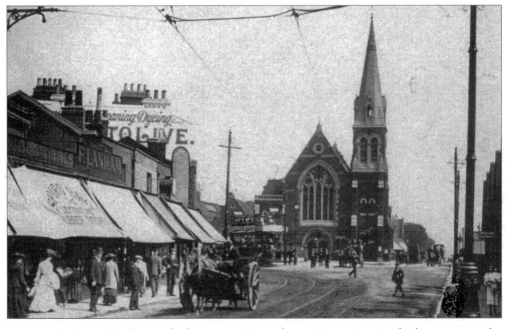

Trinity Presbyterian Church, Maryland Point, *c.* 1906. Built in 1870 opposite Maryland Point station, this church dominated Leytonstone Road. Closed in 1941, like Stratford Congregational Church, it was used for a time as a factory before it burnt down in 1953.

Pelly Road Methodist Church, Plaistow, 1903. This no-nonsense redbrick building has a complex ecclesiastical history. A Methodist mission was set up in this area of Plaistow in about 1865, with a temporary building constructed in 1868, followed by this brick building erected in 1870/1. The church was sold to Congregationalists in 1903 after a new Methodist church was built in Harold Road. The Harold Road church survived until after the Second World War, but the Congregational church only survived a few years at Pelly Road and was gone by 1909. This building then became the Given-Wilson Institute, founded in 1912 by Thomas Given-Wilson, the philanthropic vicar of St Mary's Anglican Church, Plaistow from 1884 to 1914.

DOCKS & INDUSTRY

Royal Docks from the air. The Royal Docks, one of the largest bodies of enclosed water in the world, comprising some 245 acres, developed in a piecemeal fashion. The Victoria (later Royal Victoria) Dock was completed in 1855, the Royal Albert Dock in 1880 and finally the King George V Dock, its opening delayed by the First World War until 1921. The Royals were the first docks to be directly connected to the railway system. This meant large warehouses were no longer necessary, only transit sheds, though the docks themselves indeed acted as the 'warehouse of Empire', importing raw materials from all over the world and in turn exporting a vast range of finished and manufactured goods.

Tidal Basin. This comprised the western end of the Victoria Dock, seen here bustling with barges. When it was first opened the Victoria Dock could take the largest steamships and had the latest hydraulic machinery to open the dock gates. The Victoria Dock specialized in the tobacco trade, South American beef, New Zealand lamb, citrus fruit and bananas.

Shipping in the Royal Docks from Silvertown Way. The docks were extensively rebuilt and deepened in the 1930s and new roads were built to provide better access. Silvertown Way and Silvertown bypass opened in 1934, cutting a swathe through former slums and providing a 'Road to Empire' bypassing the old level crossing bottleneck at Tidal Basin. Silvertown Way also provided a new vantage point to admire vessels in both wet and dry docks.

Grain silo, Royal Victoria Dock. The south side of the Royal Victoria Dock was once lined with great concrete grain silos, testimony to the vast amounts of corn arriving to feed London from all over the Empire. Most of these silos were built in the 1930s and '40s. They survived the Blitz but most have been demolished in recent Dockland redevelopment.

Tate's Sugar Refiner's, Silvertown, *c*. 1880. After the docks were built, the banks of the Thames and docks soon became lined with industry. This was following in the tradition of the Lea valley which had been industrialized since the Middle Ages; silk-weaving, calico-printing, tanning, as well as milling, were all important along the Lea. Because of all this industry West Ham eventually became the largest manufacturing centre in the south of England, best known for chemicals, engineering and foodstuffs. Sugar refining had been important since 1843 and Henry Tate – the main gate and general offices of his works are seen here – set up shop in Silvertown in 1877.

Produce from Tate's. Tate's principal product was white cube sugar; their nearby rivals Abram Lyle (first established in Silvertown in 1880) produced mainly golden syrup. The companies were amalgamated in 1921 to create Tate & Lyle, one of the largest sugar refiners in the world.

John Knight & Sons, Manhattan Wharf, Silvertown. Knight's 'Royal Primrose Soap Works' was established in 1880, its best known product being 'Knight's Castile' soap. The foreground of this pre-1900 photo shows wooden oil barrels from Russia piled up on the wharf in Silvertown belonging to William Simpson & Co. with the soap works in the background. These raw materials produced not only soap, but also fertilizers, glue, tallow, and even dripping.

HMS *Duncan*, Thames Ironworks, 1901. Shipbuilding is not normally associated with the Thames, but the Thames Ironworks, based at Leamouth, was a major producer of large vessels for half a century. The company originated as C.J. Mare & Co. in 1846 and built the world's first ironclad battleship, HMS *Warrior* in 1860. HMS *Duncan* (seen here just prior to launch) was completed in 1901. The launch of HMS *Albion* a few years later was the scene of a disaster when several spectators died in the backwash caused by the ship sliding into the water. Undercut by Tyneside shipyards, Thames Ironworks closed in 1912; the final ship built there was HMS *Thunderer* in 1911.

Silvertown Way under construction, 1933. Traffic congestion in Docklands was notorious as raw materials from all over world left the docks by road and rail and finished goods and manufactured products entered the docks. A major relief road, Silvertown Way, was completed in 1934, followed by the Silvertown bypass, opened in 1935, creating a broad new 'Road to Empire'.

City Mills Lock. There was also an extensive upgrading of the Lea back rivers between the wars to keep them navigable for industrial traffic (mainly barges) and for flood relief. New work completed in 1935 created this new lock to replace the old Marshgate Lock and form a new main drainage channel.

Carpenters Road Lock. A new lock was also built to connect City Mills River and Waterworks River. This was a complex operation as there was a need to keep busy roads and railways over rivers open and flowing smoothly while construction took place.

House Mill, Three Mills. This is the largest surviving water-mill in the country and is now being restored to its former glory. The Domesday Book (1086) recorded eight water-mills along the Lea. House Mill, originally owned by Stratford Langthorne Abbey, was almost certainly in existence in 1086, but the present building dates from 1776. It was built by Huguenot Daniel Bisson. The grain milled there was used to make gin as well as flour in the past.. The mill ceased production in 1941 as a result of intensive bombing.

Clock Mill, Three Mills. The House Mill and ruins of the miller's house (damaged in the Blitz, but recently restored as a visitor centre) can be seen behind and to the left of the oast house roof of the House Mill. Barges can be seen moored against the mill, which was built in 1817.

Stratford Railway Works, 1864. Stratford was formerly a great railway town; the Great Eastern Railway's main works were created there and built up under George Hudson, the charismatic 'Railway King'. The works occupied a vast site of some 78 acres with 6,000 employees building locomotives and carriages and everything associated with railways, from tickets at their own printing works to cutlery. In this early photo several Gooch 2-4-0s can be seen under construction.

West Ham Brewery, Romford Road, c. 1902. There were once numerous brewers in West Ham, notably Savill Brothers of Maryland Road. Despite this vast advertising hoarding West Ham Brewery was a short-lived works.

Bonallack's Carriage Works, Stratford Broadway, adjacent to Stratford Town Hall. This began life before 1839 as Stephen Gowar & Co., which was taken over by Bonallack's carriage-builders in 1886. The company later moved with the times to build car bodies, based in Forest Gate. West Ham Corporation meanwhile acquired the Broadway works and converted them into Stratford Fire Station in 1910.

Tonic Sol-Fa Printing Works, Plaistow. There is a long tradition of printing in West Ham, particularly along the Lea, though the Tonic Sol-Fa was rather a different concern. John Curwen had popularized the Tonic Sol-Fa system of musical notation and founded the Tonic Sol-Fa Press in the former Plaistow Congregational Church (built in 1807) to popularize it further. Later the company became the Curwen Press and gained a reputation as a high-quality art publisher.

Abbey Mills Pumping Station. The station was opened in 1868 as part of the Northern Outfall Sewer scheme, which had been designed by Joseph Bazalgette to channel London's sewage out of the capital into the Thames at Beckton.

Interior of Abbey Mills Pumping Station, 1869. This engraving shows details of the spectacular cast-iron interior architecture. The sewage was originally pumped by four vast beam engines, though these have since been replaced by rather more prosaic diesel engines.

West Ham Pumping Station. Despite the Northern Outfall Sewer crossing the borough, West Ham's sewage system was not actually connected to it until after 1893 and the corporation had to make separate arrangements for sewage disposal. West Ham Pumping Station was completed in 1901 to pump sewage up into the high-level Outfall Sewer.

Canning Town Generating Station, Quadrant Street, *c.* 1905. West Ham was a pioneer in the production of municipal electricity, starting as early as 1895. The principal need for electricity was not originally domestic, but to power tramways and street lighting. Canning Town Generating Station was officially opened in April 1905.

Interior of Canning Town Generating Station, *c.* 1905. The original capacity of the plant was 9,100 hp. Between the wars there was of course a dramatic rise in demand for domestic electricity and capacity was accordingly increased drastically. The borough's power undertaking was nationalized in 1947.

HOUSES

Ham House. This began life as Grove House, and was known as Rooke Hall by the sixteenth century. Between 1762 and 1780 it was owned by Dr Fothergill who created a magnificent botanical garden, one of the finest in Europe. In the nineteenth century the property was owned by the Quaker banking family the Gurneys. The house was demolished in 1872, and the grounds were sold in 1874 to form West Ham Park — the site of the house is marked by a cairn.

Upton House. Situated on the opposite side of Upton Lane to Ham House, which was also, confusingly, known as Upton House for a short time in the eighteenth century. It was typical of a number of fine seventeenth- and eighteenth-century houses built in West Ham as country retreats for City merchants and businessmen. Upton House was rebuilt in 1731 and was the birthplace of (Lord) Joseph Lister (1827–1912), the founder of antiseptic surgery. It was demolished in 1968.

Cumberland House and barn. This stood in Elkington Road off New Barn Street and dated back to at least the seventeenth century. It took its name from the Duke of Cumberland (George III's younger brother) who owned the house between 1787 and 1790. The building was demolished in 1935. The barn on the right of the picture probably dated back to the sixteenth century, perhaps even earlier as it was said to have been Stratford Langthorne Abbey's tithe barn. It was undoubtedly one of the biggest in Essex, though unfortunately it had fallen down by 1905.

Hyde House, Plaistow. The engraving shows the gateway of Hyde House which had the date '1579' engraved on it together with the motto 'This is the gate of Everlasting Life'. According to tradition, the monks from Stratford Langthorne Abbey lived at Hyde House after the Dissolution. The house itself was a sixteenth-century weatherboarded building, the home of Sir Thomas Foot (died 1688), Lord Mayor of London, and later Aaron Hill (1685–1750), eccentric poet and playwright who earned local ridicule after trying to produce wine from a vineyard in the grounds. Hyde House was demolished in about 1810, though the gate survived until 1859.

Old Houses in Balaam Street. Plaistow retained a village-like atmosphere well into the twentieth century. Although it is hard to visualize the village green now, it occupied the area now bounded by High Street, Richmond Street, and North Street, but is now completely built over. Balaam Street (locally pronounced Bay-lam not Bar-lam) has had many distinguished residents, including: Luke Howard (1772–1864), the founder of scientific meteorology; Edmund Burke (1729–97), statesman; Aaron Hill (see p. 42); George Edwards (1693–1773), the founder of modern ornithology; and Dr William Dodd (1729–77), the dandified curate who was hanged for forgery after a case which scandalized high society.

Pawnbrokers' Almshouses, Woodgrange Road, Forest Gate. With no social security in the Victorian period, the old who were no longer able to work were reliant on family or charity. Almshouses gave some security for the few lucky enough to obtain a place and they were once numerous in West Ham. In this engraving we see the almshouses built by the Pawnbrokers' Charitable Institution in 1849, in 'Elizabethan' style. These buildings housed up to eight poor of the parish until their demolition in 1898.

Almshouses in Church Passage, West Ham. Originating in 1636 from a bequest by one John Newman, these almshouses were rebuilt between 1745 and 1748 by a further bequest from James Cooper. This terrace was demolished in 1944.

INNS

*The Swan, Stratford Broadway. This early photo predates the building of Stratford Town Hall in 1869.
There was an inn called the Swan as early as 1631 and this structure was probably eighteenth century in
origin. It was once an important coaching stop, the last before London, and later became a tram terminus.
The pub was demolished and rebuilt in 1925.*

The Spotted Dog at Upton. This inn is the oldest secular building in West Ham, comprising a timber-framed and weatherboard building of the sixteenth century or earlier with nineteenth-century brick additions. Traditionally it was named because it was once the kennels of Henry VIII's hunting dogs, which is entirely plausible. The Spotted Dog was noted in the nineteenth century, when it was still a pleasant rural retreat, for its tea gardens and cricket ground.

The Pigeons, Romford Road, before 1885. A large wagon stands outside this historic pub which has been in existence since at least 1776. It was earlier known as the Three Pigeons and once had a windmill standing beside it, though this was demolished in 1860. The pub itself was rebuilt in about 1898.

The Angel, Church Street, West Ham, 1902. This was a timber-framed building dating back to the sixteenth or seventeenth century, but rebuilt in 1910.

The King of Prussia, Stratford Broadway, 1904. This pub was patriotically renamed the King Edward VII in 1914 and was probably built in the mid-eighteenth century, with its original name commemorating Frederick the Great, King of Prussia, 1740–86.

SECTION SIX

PEOPLE

The burning of the Stratford Martyrs, 1556. Thirteen Protestants were burnt at the stake on 27 June 1556 on Stratford Green, which stretched from where St John's Church now stands in Stratford Broadway to the University of East London campus in Romford Road. A monument to the martyrs was erected in 1879 and their names are commemorated in several Beckton street names.

George Edwards (1694–1773). He lived in
Balaam Street, Plaistow and was known as the
'Father of modern ornithology' and wrote a
monumental four-volume treatise, *The History
of Birds*, listing every species known then and a
further three-volume work, *Gleanings in
Natural History*, with 600 hand-coloured
prints. He was a member of both the Royal
Society and Society of Antiquaries.

Aaron Hill (1685–1750). He lived in Hyde
House in Plaistow, then considered a country
house in a remote village. Nominally a
dramatist, Hill earned notoriety through his
overblown poetry and plays, which were
widely ridiculed when performed. He earned
local mockery too when he planted a vineyard;
his attempts to make wine without bothering
to include the fermentation process were, not
surprisingly, a resounding failure.

Dick Turpin (1705–39). This notorious Essex highwayman had many reputed local links. It was claimed that he rustled cattle and horses as a young man in Plaistow Marsh and also reputedly escaped from pursuers across the Thames at Prince Regent Ferry (now Silvertown). It was also said that he once lived at Richmond Street, Plaistow and married an East Ham girl named Palmer. Most of the legends about Turpin's life are simply legends and far from being a gentleman highwayman he was a very brutal mugger, burglar, and murderer.

Edmund Burke (1729–97). Burke was one of the great statesmen, orators and writers of the Georgian Age. He lived in Brunstock Cottage, Balaam Street, Plaistow between 1759 and 1761 and received a stream of distinguished visitors while staying there.

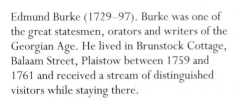

Elizabeth Fry (1780–1845). Founder of the prison reform movement and prominent Quaker, Elizabeth Fry lived for a time at The Cedars (now demolished) in Portway. Here, in 1842, she received a visit from Frederick King of Prussia which was the subject of huge local celebrations though Elizabeth herself was modest about her achievements.

Joseph, Lord Lister (1827–1912). The founder of antiseptic surgery, Lister was born in Upton House, Upton Lane. He received the Honorary Freedom of the Borough in 1908.

John Curwen (1816–80). John Curwen popularized the Tonic Sol-Fa form of musical notation which taught thousands if not millions to appreciate and participate in music. He established both the Tonic Sol-Fa College in Forest Gate and the Tonic Sol-Fa Press in Plaistow. He was minister at Plaistow Congregationalist Church, Balaam Street from 1844 to 1864.

John Meeson. First Mayor of West Ham, 1886–7, he served on West Ham Council between 1886 and 1890. Before that he had been chairman of the Local Board from 1863 to 1875. Meeson was a significant local cement manufacturer.

Alderman William Crow. One of West Ham's civic fathers, Crow owned a major Stratford jewellery business. A member of the original municipal council created in 1886, he remained on the council until 1929 and served twice as mayor, 1895–6 and 1913–14. He was presented with the Honorary Freedom of the Borough in 1931 'in recognition of distinguished public services rendered'.

Frederic Hilleary. Clerk to West Ham Local Board from 1874, Frederic Hilleary was a prominent Stratford solicitor and appointed first West Ham Town Clerk in 1886, serving honourably until 1913 with 'unfailing courtesy, loyalty and tact'.

West Ham's first Borough Council, 1886–7. Top row, left to right: Councillors W. Crow, T. Knight, T. Anderson, A. Govier, J.H. Pavitt, W. Lewis, C. Mansfield, H. Wagstaff, J. Cook. Second row: Councillors H. Young, J. Maw, E. Fulcher, R. Fielder, E. Jex, S. Vinicombe, E. E. Barnett, J. H. Bethell, F. Hammersley. Third row: Councillors G. H. Courtney, W. Hands, G. W. Kidd, R. Wortley, H. Callaghan, R. White, W. H. Medcalf, M. Adamson, F. Smith. Seated: Aldermen H. Phillips, J. Scully, W. Deason, G. Hay, J. Meeson (Mayor), G. Rivett, H. Worland, C. Stoner, H. Barry, R. L. Curtis.

West Ham Borough Council, 1935–6. Front row, left to right: Aldermen Mrs D. Parsons, T.E. Groves, J.T. Scoulding, T. Wooder, W.T. Bell, J.T. Husband, J.J. Jones, W.J. Thorne , Councillor Cuthbert Collins (Mayor), Aldermen G. Groot, B.W. Gardner, E.J. Reed, J.H. Hollins, W.J. Reed, H.J. Rumsey, G.R. Blaker, Alderman Mrs E. Bock (Deputy Mayor). Second row: Councillors A.J. Walker, G.J. Stokes, J. Doherty, A.W. Wells, D.W. Hall, C.A. Bennett, W.H. Luscombe, E.W. Wordley, W.C. Ridgwell, A.E. Cresswell, G. Doherty, Mrs E.J. Gregory, E.W. White, C.H. Ward, H.J. Manners, Mrs E.C. Cook. Third row: Councillors A.G. Schirn, W.A. Gillman, A.C. Gentry, Mrs E.E. Whybrew, E.F. Bradley, Mrs A.A. Barnes, A.G. Gay, F.E. Mansford, Mrs J.A. Hollins, F.A. Warner, Mrs F.A. Wood, P. Hearn, Mrs F. Harris, S.M. Edwards, E.C. Cannon, E.H.J. Adams. Back row: Councillors A.E. Harnwell, G.A. Taylor, S. Lee, E.J. Fox, A.C. Moorey, C.K. Collins, W.P. Foley, Mrs E. Venton, D. Thorogood, G.J Smith, A.B. Macgregor, M.J. Sullivan, Mrs A.M. Clark.

Keir Hardie (1856–1915), the first ever Labour Member of Parliament, was elected in 1892 for the West Ham South constituency. The son of a Scottish miner, Hardie caused outrage by going to Parliament in a cloth cap and workman's suit. Defeated in West Ham three years later in 1895, he later served as MP for Merthyr Tydfil. He was also the first Chairman of the Parliamentary Labour Party.

Will Thorne (1887–1946). Dominating West Ham politics for half a century, Thorne originally worked as a stoker in Beckton Gasworks and was taught to read and write by Eleanor Marx. A political firebrand, he founded the Gas Workers and General Labourers Union in 1889, was elected to West Ham Council in 1891, elected MP for West Ham South in 1906 and served in that capacity until 1945. He was President of the TUC in 1912.

West Ham Parish Church Choir, *c.* 1936. In the centre seated is the vicar, the Revd A.W.W. Wallace, flanked by his two curates, on the left the Revd A. Weir. Behind with glasses and hood is Sydney Campbell, organist from 1931 to 1937 then organist at Ely, Southwark and Canterbury Cathedrals, and St George's Chapel, Windsor. Other choristers include Messrs Brand, Glander, Hill, Hudson, Langford, Newell, Roberts, Sparks and Walmsley.

Daisy Parsons (1890–1957), seen here presenting school prizes. Having been arrested as a suffragette in 1914, she was the first woman Mayor of West Ham and served as a councillor for thirty years, earning a formidable reputation as a political debater. She was awarded the MBE in 1951 for public service.

Shadrack's Coal Yard, Barking Road. This is a rare photograph of ordinary working men at their day's work. However, they are not actually working as they have stopped to listen to an itinerant preacher giving a Bible reading. The date of the photograph is unknown, but Shadrack's was a prominent local coal merchant's between the wars.

PUBLIC SERVICES

Stratford Town Hall. West Ham became a municipal borough in 1886 and a county borough three years later in 1889. By 1869, however, when West Ham was still only administered by a local board, that board had already recognized the rapid growth of the area and commissioned a splendid new town hall. The fire station next door was opened in 1877, now converted into offices. The town hall was lavishly restored in 1986 for the borough's centenary.

NEW TOWNHALL, STRATFORD, ESSEX.

Engraving of Stratford Town Hall. The *Illustrated London News* for 18 September 1869 carried a long laudatory article praising the architecture of the newly-completed town hall at Stratford, together with this fine engraving. The town hall stands on the site of a group of tumbledown timber-framed buildings which included the Albion Coffee House, a popular local meeting place.

Stratford Town Hall, 1906.

West Ham coat of arms. Granted in 1886, the arms summarize the borough's heritage. The ship represents the docks, the hammers industry. The crozier represents Stratford Langthorne Abbey, the chevrons the Montfichet arms (William de Montfichet founded Stratford Langthorne Abbey in 1135). These arms were eventually adopted for the new London Borough of Newham created in 1965 through the union of the former county boroughs of East Ham and West Ham.

West Ham civic regalia. The mayor and mayoress's chains, featuring the borough coat of arms and names of previous mayors.

A splendid photograph of West Ham's horse-drawn fire engine and crew, c. 1870. The local board fire brigade was formed in 1858, though it did not become professional until 1877–8. The first motor fire engine was purchased in 1909, though horse-drawn tenders were still in use as late as 1923. In the interwar years many West Ham firemen were former navy men.

Canning Town Fire Station, *c.* 1906. Built in 1877–8, this grand yellow-brick edifice in Barking Road was demolished in 1970.

A West Ham Fire Brigade rescue tender from 1936.

School board offices, Stratford. The school board was founded in 1871 in response to the Education Act of 1871; the earlier voluntary educational schemes including the National Schools and British Schools had never been able to cope with the vast demand of the rapidly-growing housing estates, and the new board immediately faced a huge building programme. These offices were later used for the Education and Borough Treasurer's Departments.

West Ham Technical Institute. The institute opened in 1898 with departments offering courses in science, engineering and art. There was also a separate women's department. In 1921 the institute was renamed West Ham Municipal College and underwent further expansion and change after the Second World War, first becoming West Ham College of Technology, then forming part of North East London Polytechnic. In 1992 the polytechnic took university status and became the University of East London.

Queen Mary's Hospital, West Ham Lane, c. 1925. This much-loved local institution originated as a dispensary in 1861. The hospital was first built in 1890, then rebuilt and extended in 1895 and again between 1906 and 1910. The name was changed to honour Queen Mary during the First World War in 1916. Seriously damaged in the Blitz, but repaired and reopened, the hospital was finally closed in 1984, to be demolished in 1987 and replaced by a housing estate.

Plaistow Fever Hospital, Western Road. This scene shows parents greeting children at the gates. A hospital was first opened on this site in 1871 by West Ham Poor Law Union as a smallpox hospital. It was rebuilt between 1899 and 1902 as a municipal hospital for infectious diseases. Bombed in the Blitz, it nevertheless survived to become an annexe of Queen Mary's Hospital in 1947, though it has since closed.

Stratford Central Library, Water Lane. West Ham was the second borough in Essex to adopt the Public Libraries Act, with local teachers playing an important part in the adoption. The borough's first temporary library was situated in Rokeby House, Stratford Broadway in 1892. The new Central Library, shown here, was opened in October 1898 adjacent to the new Technical Institute and was paid for by 'Whisky Money' (a portion of the Port of London's excise duty reserved for public benefit).

Plaistow Library, North Street. This branch was opened by Andrew Carnegie in 1903; the philanthropist Passmore Edwards paid £4,000 for the library to be built.

Passmore Edwards Museum. The museum served for nearly a century as a repository for natural history and archaeological material from all over Essex. This striking interior view, probably taken in the Edwardian period, shows both the upper and ground floor collections set out around the rotunda. The museum was closed by Newham Council in 1994.

Passmore Edwards Museum, Romford Road. The museum was opened by Daisy, Countess of Warwick in 1900 to house the collections of the Essex Field Club. The museum was built as part of the complex including the West Ham Technical Institute and Central Library.

Balaam Street Baths. Public baths provision was very important in an overcrowded borough in which many houses were built without proper sanitary facilities. Balaam Street Baths were opened in 1901 and featured two swimming pools as well as public bathing facilities. In the interwar years the baths were famous as the home of Plaistow United Swimming Club, which bred many champion and Olympic swimmers including E.H. Temme, the first man to swim the Channel in both directions.

West Ham Generating Station, Canning Town. West Ham first began municipal electrical generation in 1895. This Quadrant Street plant opened in 1904. West Ham Council vigorously promoted the use of electricity, at first for industrial use then in the interwar years for domestic application. The council electrical undertaking was nationalized in 1947.

30,000 kilowatt turbo-alternator, West Ham Generating Station. The West Ham municipal electrical supply undertaking was one of the largest in the country and surplus electricity produced at the station was sold on at a profit to the National Grid after the creation of the grid in 1934.

SCHOOLS

West Ham Church School. Before the Education Act of 1870 a variety of dame schools and church schools provided some education, though coverage was patchy and inadequate. West Ham Church School was one of the oldest, founded in 1723 as a charitable institution. At first lessons were held in the church itself, but now take place in more modern surroundings! (The present school, built in 1964, stands in Portway.) This photograph shows Group 7 in 1897.

South Hallsville Board School, Canning Town. Founded in 1878, this was one of the first schools to be built by the new West Ham School Board, itself founded in 1871. The school was located in Agate Street in the heart of a very poor district. The school will always be associated with one of the worst disasters of the Blitz when it suffered a direct hit. Tragically local families were sheltering there while waiting for evacuation and seventy-six people were killed. This photograph dates from 1897.

Abbey Road Board School, West Ham. This school opened in 1881 for 800 pupils. Closed in 1938, it was demolished in 1946. The photograph shows Group VII in 1885.

New City Road School, Plaistow, c. 1913. Opened in 1897, this is a typical brick-built three-decker school. It was built in an isolated part of the borough so, although it had places for 1,560 pupils, the school roll was not filled for some years.

Park School, Eleanor Road, West Ham. Opened in 1889 as West Ham Park Board School, it had 1,366 pupils by 1897. This photograph dates from 1910.

Napier Road School, West Ham. Another evocative classroom scene taken shortly after the school opened in 1904.

SHOPS & SHOPPING

Angel Lane Market, 1954. Stratford has been a regionally important shopping centre throughout the twentieth century, featuring large department stores such as Boardman's and Roberts together with many smaller but equally well-recalled establishments and above all Angel Lane Market. Remembered by many, this noisy, cheerful and rumbustious market went on late into the night, its stalls lit by naphtha flares and oil lamps. Now only a memory thanks to the comprehensive redevelopment of Stratford in the 1970s, the very name of Angel Lane has disappeared. A smaller covered market survives in Stratford Shopping Centre.

Market stalls in Stratford Broadway. Market traders set up their stalls in Stratford Broadway from 1858 onwards. Recently the street market has undergone a revival as a speciality craft market. This photograph was taken on Saturday 2 May 1925 on the south side of Broadway.

West Ham Lane, 1902. Although Stratford Broadway was the focus of shopping, there were also shops in West Ham Lane running down to West Ham parish church. Note the post office, then the row of timber buildings (possibly of seventeenth-century origin – now all demolished) including Bradley's grocery, an 'Oyster Bar' and Ablett the undertaker.

Rathbone Market. Like Angel Lane Market, this Canning Town market originated when traders simply set up stalls, in this case along the Victoria Dock Road in the 1880s. As traffic increased the stalls later moved to nearby Rathbone Street, seen here, c. 1925.

Rathbone Market, c. 1935. The market soon spilled over into Barking Road as its popularity increased; Canning Town Public Hall can be seen in the background of this photograph. The whole area was redeveloped in 1963 with the building of Canning Town flyover. The market was moved permanently into a small windswept plot in Barking Road opposite the Royal Oak tavern and is now the only surviving traditional open-air market left in Newham.

Green Street, *c.* 1904. This is an ancient thoroughfare – the name was known at least as early as the time of Elizabeth I – which marks the boundary between East and West Ham. It is also the site of a market and busy shopping street, now best known for its lively Asian market.

Queens Road Market. In about 1900 many Green Street market traders moved to Queens Road, off Green Street, and thrived there throughout the first half of the twentieth century. Following redevelopment the stallholders were located to a purpose-built covered market off Green Street in about 1970.

61–77 Upton Lane. Upton is another distinctive neighbourhood focused on Upton Lane and its grand Victorian parade of shops. This photograph was taken on the corner of Studley Road.

Shops at 73–75 Upton Lane, July 1902. This close-up shows Moran's and Wiedhofft's. There were many German immigrants in West Ham before the First World War – indeed the borough had a policy of attracting skilled German engineers to its industries – but German-sounding shops and businesses were damaged in anti-German riots, particularly after the sinking of the *Lusitania*. Many Germans anglicized their names to avoid attack.

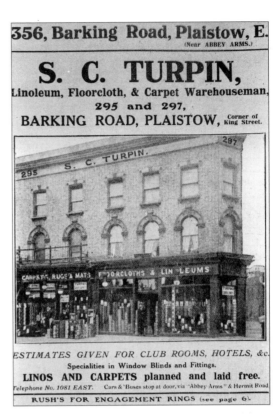

356, Barking Road, Plaistow, E.
(Near ABBEY ARMS.)

S. C. TURPIN,

Linoleum, Floorcloth, & Carpet Warehouseman,
295 and 297,
BARKING ROAD, PLAISTOW, Corner of King Street.

ESTIMATES GIVEN FOR CLUB ROOMS, HOTELS, &c.
Specialities in Window Blinds and Fittings.
LINOS AND CARPETS planned and laid free.
Telephone No. 1081 EAST. Cars & 'Buses stop at door, via 'Abbey Arms" & Hermit Road
RUSH'S FOR ENGAGEMENT RINGS (see page 6).

Turpin's, Barking Road, 1909. This prominent carpet and lino shop is still a feature of Barking Road, located on the corner of King Street.

Stone's, 231 Hermit Road, Canning Town, *c.* 1895. Another shop located on a narrow corner site, this photograph shows an archetypical grocery.

Larkin's of Canning Town, *c.* 1910. The Larkins were a well-known shopkeeping family in East and West Ham. Henry Larkin was known as 'The Peanut King' as he was one of the earliest roasted peanut sellers. This picture shows the Larkin's fruiterers shop at 39 Freemasons Road.

SECTION TEN

SOCIAL LIFE

Borough Theatre, Stratford, c. 1896. This photograph was taken shortly after the theatre's opening. Designed by Frank Matcham, it hosted many famous performers including Ellen Terry, Sir Henry Irving and Beerbohm Tree. The Borough was the largest theatre in Essex and one of the largest in the metropolitan area; it seated over 3,000. Converted into the Rex Cinema in 1933, it was closed in 1969 and at the time of writing there are ambitious plans for restoration. Stratford had several theatres and music halls, the most famous being the Theatre Royal. Opened in 1884, it was made famous after 1953 by the residency of Joan Littlewood's Theatre Workshop which produced a string of gritty bittersweet hits such as A Taste of Honey, Oh What a Lovely War! *and* Sparrows Can't Sing.

Borough Theatre, *c.* 1905. *The Sins of London* is playing; a tantalizing title indeed!

Green Gate Cinema. Opened in 1911 and enlarged in 1921, the Green Gate's name was changed to the Rio in 1953 and closed in 1957. The building survives as a snooker club. This view dates from about 1920 when the film showing was *Kilties Three*, a First World War adventure film. Cinema was one of most popular forms of entertainment in West Ham with no less than nineteen operating in West Ham when this photograph was taken.

Canning Town Public Hall. The hall was opened in 1894 in Barking Road to serve as the administrative centre for Canning Town and the populous south of the borough. A wide range of public functions and events took place in and outside the hall, which was beautifully restored for its centenary in 1994.

Canning Town Public Hall, *c.* 1905. Another view showing buildings to the west. Immediately to left of the public hall is Canning Town Library, opened in 1893 by philanthropist Passmore Edwards; this was the borough's first permanent public library. Also in view is the London & Provincial Bank, on the corner.

West Ham Park, *c.* 1918. This park originated in the sixteenth century as the grounds of Grove House, later Rookes Hall and later still known as Ham House. In that incarnation it was made famous by the eminent surgeon Dr John Fothergill, who in the eighteenth century turned it into one of the greatest botanical gardens in Europe. Ham House was demolished in 1872 with the site marked by the cairn of stones which can be seen in the centre of the photograph.

West Ham Park. Another view from the Edwardian period. In the nineteenth century Ham House was owned by the Gurney family, a prominent local Quaker family, who sold it in 1874 for use as a public park. Unusually the park is managed not by the borough but by the Corporation of London. In this photograph West Hammers enjoy a Sunday stroll or just sit quietly under a parasol.

West Ham Park. Many of the fine arboreta established by Fothergill survive to ornament the gardens today.

Canning Town Recreation Ground. Better known locally as Beckton Park, it was opened in 1894, one of the first public parks to be run by West Ham Corporation. It was an important 'green lung' for the overcrowded south of the borough.

Lyle Park was almost the only official open space in West Silvertown, a long narrow park squeezed in between the factories and their wharves, but offering unparalleled views of the Thames and its shipping. A drinking fountain in the park forms the touching memorial to the war dead of West Silvertown.

Charabanc outing. After the First World War the roads to Southend-on-Sea, Clacton and Margate were packed with charabancs in the summer months. Many social groups organized such outings, including temperance societies. This was clearly not a teetotal trip as it left from the Spread Eagle pub on the corner of St Stephen's Road and Manor Road!

Hop picking. Each August and September there was a huge exodus from West Ham and East London as families made their way down to Kent to help gather the hop harvest. Going 'Opping' formed an extended and often the only holiday for many working people. In the hopfields the hop-pickers lived in purpose-built, if basic, huts and older residents recall both hard work to gather hops (earning money by the bushel) and the happy atmosphere of parties round bonfires under the stars.

Christmas party at the Coloured Men's Institute, 1926. There has been a large black and Asian community in south West Ham ever since the mid-Victorian period, a legacy of the docks in their role as 'Gateway of Empire' and their vast worldwide trade. During the Depression in the 1920s and 1930s blacks faced hardship and discrimination, so a Ceylonese minister, Pastor Chunchie, opened the Coloured Men's Institute in Tidal Basin Road as a social and support centre.

SPORTS

West Ham United, 1900–1. This famous team was founded in 1900 from three amateur teams: St Luke's, Thames Ironworks and the Old Castle Swifts. Arnold Hills, philanthropic owner of Thames Ironworks, donated enough money for these teams to merge and go professional. West Ham's nickname 'The Hammers' derives from the sledgehammers used in Thames Ironworks.

West Ham United, 1922–3. By 1923 West Ham had been promoted to the First Division and got as far as the Cup Final, which was the first to be played at Wembley Stadium. West Ham played Bolton and lost 2–0, but still received heroes' welcomes on their return.

The 1923 Cup Final attracted a gate of 150,000, far more than the stadium could cope with and the crowd spilled on to the pitch. PC Scorey, mounted on a white horse, helped push back spectators behind the lines so that the game could start. It was all done with good humour and PC Scorey became a hero.

North West Ham Athletic and Boxing Club, *c.* 1925. There is a long tradition of boxing in West Ham; even in the eighteenth century illegal prizefighting took place on the marshes. Jem Mace (1831–1910), world heavyweight champion, lived in Stratford and Billy Wells (1887–1967), British heavyweight boxing champion 1911–19, lived in Forest Gate. In the early part of this century the borough produced many flyweight and other lightweight champions.

West Ham Memorial Ground, 1903. Arnold Hills also paid for the building of West Ham Memorial Ground, which was opened in 1897 in Canning Town. This had the longest swimming pool in Britain and the fastest banked cycle racing track in the country. This photograph shows a National Cycle Union meet in 1903.

West Ham Memorial Ground, 1904. The Shaftesbury Cycling Club 10 mile championship race, 20 August 1904.

Shaftesbury Cycling Club. Seen here in 1905, pre-lycra days but still sportingly attired.

Thames Ironworks Cycling Club. In this 1895 view the behatted gents of the club are about to cycle off on an evening run culminating in refreshments at the Balaclava pub in Wanstead.

Motorcycle race at West Ham Memorial Ground. These early machines were heavy and difficult to manoeuvre at speed, so accidents were common. Despite this, cloth caps were the only protective headgear worn! This photograph shows a 5 mile handicap race, date unknown.

Speedway at West Ham Stadium. Opened in 1928, West Ham Stadium was the home ground of the West Ham speedway team, one of the country's best. This photograph shows the West Ham Mayor (Alderman Ted Wooder) reopening the stadium in April 1940; it had been closed in 1939 as a war precaution and was closed again in September 1940 when the Blitz began.

Speedway race at West Ham Stadium, April 1940. The stadium could hold 40,000. It was later used as a track for greyhound racing and closed in 1972. A housing estate was built over the site, its street names commemorating famous speedway stars.

STREETS & VIEWS

THE BROADWAY, STRATFORD.

Stratford Broadway, north side, c. 1912. A policeman marches purposefully towards the camera in this busy scene. On the left is St John's Church with the dome of Stratford Town Hall beyond, while the Coach and Horses (no longer in existence) stands on the right.

Gurney monument, Stratford Broadway, 1915. The obelisk on the left was erected by public subscription in memory of Samuel Gurney (died 1856), a philanthropic local scion of the prominent Quaker banking family. A No.10 London General omnibus is on its way to the Elephant & Castle.

General view of Stratford Broadway, 1925. Crowds have gathered on the pavement outside the Angel Inn, while to the right a No. 63 London Transport tram is passing through Stratford on its way from Ilford to London.

Stratford Broadway, with horse omnibus on the north side, 1895.

Stratford Broadway, north side looking towards the town hall, c. 1898. Horse trams approach each other. Bonallack's can be seen next to the town hall; this large local company were carriage-builders and later switched to making motor car bodies.

Stratford Broadway, south side looking towards the town hall. This view dates from about 1907 and shows the tram terminus outside the Swan on the left. The men on the right are checking job vacancies, which were pasted up daily on the church noticeboard of St John's.

Stratford Broadway, horse omnibus terminus outside the Swan. In this earlier view the tram terminus can be seen to have had its origins as a horse omnibus terminus.

Stratford Broadway, cabmen's shelter, *c.* 1895. Cabmen also halted at the Swan and pose here beside their shelter. The Swan had in fact been a staging post for centuries and was the last important inn before crossing the Lea into Middlesex.

The Grove, Stratford, 1904. A fairly humble parade of shops on the right. The poet Gerard Manley Hopkins was born in this street in 1844.

Angel Lane, Stratford. Earlier mention has already been made of this thriving market (see p. 69); this view, however, shows a forlorn scene of near-emptiness, perhaps taken after the end of the day's trading or on a Sunday.

Stratford High Street in the General Strike, 1926. Crowds mill excitedly on the pavement as a convoy of vehicles under police guard heads towards London. The George no longer exists and, across the road, the Empire cinema with its distinctive obelisk on the roof has also been demolished.

Stratford High Street and Borough Theatre. A more peaceful scene, *c.* 1905. Stratford High Street originated as a causeway between Stratford Broadway and Bow Bridge. In the Edwardian era it was a thriving street of shops, but more recently it has effectively become an urban motorway.

The Old Dispensary, Romford Road. Built between 1690 and 1720, this weatherboarded house is one of the oldest secular buildings in West Ham. In the 1860s it housed a dispensary, but after 1885 it became the headquarters of Webb's builders and shopfitters. More recently it has housed offices of the Newham Museum Service and Stratford City Challenge team.

Romford Road, Stratford, *c.* 1900. A rather dreary view taken from opposite the Old Dispensary, looking towards St John's Church.

Romford Road, Stratford, *c.* 1905. The same view a few years later; poles carrying tram cables have been erected. West Ham Corporation Tramways began running electric trams in 1904.

Romford Road, Forest Gate, *c.* 1907. A westbound tram makes its way along this tree-lined street rather more sedately than the pace of today's traffic would allow! The twin spires of Woodgrange Baptist Church (built in 1882) can be seen in the distance. This was a fairly well-to-do area, but unexpectedly suffered a minor riot in 1880, when windows were smashed by crowds protesting against poverty.

Barking Road near the Abbey Arms, looking east, *c.* 1908.

Barking Road, 1930. In the distance the huge roof of the Grand Cinema can be seen on the right-hand side of the road. Opened in 1913, the cinema was badly damaged in the Blitz and later demolished.

Woodgrange Road, Forest Gate. This busy street, Forest Gate's main shopping thoroughfare, originated as a country lane leading to Epping Forest and at one time there actually was a 'forest gate' across the road to keep out straying cattle.

The Broadway, Woodgrange Road, Forest Gate. This view dates from about 1898 and shows the row of shops known as the Broadway at the corner of Woodgrange Road and Forest Lane. The most prominent shop is Pattison's Toy Bazaar, while the (surviving) fountain and clock make a rather gaudy traffic island.

Woodgrange Road, Forest Gate. Another view of shops in Woodgrange Road this time near the railway bridge. The rather confusingly named Wanstead Park station is out of sight to the left; Wanstead Park is actually some distance away. The furniture shop on the left has a remarkable collection of hire-purchase advertisements.

Woodgrange Road, Forest Gate, 1902. Spratt's draper's is on the right, with the grand spires of the
Wesleyan Methodist Church and its hall beyond. The church had the biggest congregation in West Ham
(excluding Roman Catholic churches) when this photograph was taken. The church was rebuilt in 1962
following extensive Blitz damage.

Earlham Grove, Forest Gate. A more peaceful scene from about 1906. This quiet residential street is
typical of much of Forest Gate, with larger detached houses mainly built in the late Victorian period. On
the right Earlham Hall can be seen, an important public facility.

Forest Lane and Woodgrange Road, Forest Gate, *c.* 1905. Another view of the Broadway parade of shops; the ornate clock-cum-drinking fountain can be seen on the right, while a steam lorry stands in front of the Railway Tavern.

The Portway. West Ham Park stands on the left, with a keeper's cottage at the gateway.

Another view of the same area, *c.* 1905. A family making its way into the park passes an ice cream stall.

Leytonstone Road, looking towards Maryland Point, 1909. Ornate Edwardian shop fronts with Trinity Presbyterian Church beyond, built in 1870 and demolished in 1953 after several ignominious years as a furniture factory. Maryland Point took its name from the American state of Maryland, the name being brought back in the mid-seventeenth century by Richard Lee who had an estate there, but later settled near Stratford and named his estate in honour of his American property.

Balaam Street, Plaistow. The curious name is an ancient one; it was known as early as 1371 and was taken from the local Balame or Balun family.

Balaam Street, Plaistow, 1933.

St Mary's Road, Plaistow. A view of the long-surviving old cottages which once gave a village-like feel to this road and its environs.

Humberstone Road, Plaistow, *c.* 1913. This view is typical of many Plaistow streets. Long terraces of fairly good quality houses were built in the mid-nineteenth century for artisans, journeymen and clerks.

Kingsland Road, Plaistow. Another similar street nearby; notice the lack of traffic!

Green Street. This busy shopping street forms the boundary between East and West Ham. It is an ancient thoroughfare; there is a reference to 'Grene Lane' as far back as 1527. It may even have been the lane along which Thomas Plantagenet, Duke of Gloucester, was conveyed to his death in 1397 on the orders of his nephew Richard II. The northern end was earlier known as Gipsy Lane.

Upton Park Road, *c.* 1905. This street formed part of the Upton Manor estate, developed for housing from 1852 onwards.

West Ham Lane, *c.* 1953. Queen Mary's Hospital can be seen on the left with a shopping parade on the right. Stratford Town Hall stands in the distance.

Abbey Road, *c.* 1890. This was the heart of West Ham village when it was still a village.

The various Docklands Settlements around the borough – philanthropic institutions set up by churches, public schools and charitable bodies – formed almost self-contained communities. This settlement, dating from 1894 and originating as the Malvern College Mission, developed after the Second World War into the Mayflower Centre.

Bow flyover, *c.* 1968. Shown here shortly after completion, a stark concrete structure that could hardly have been imagined by Queen Maud when she ordered the building of the first Bow Bridge 850 years earlier!

Iron Bridge, Canning Town. This was until recently the lowest crossing of the Lea. Built in 1810, it formed part of the Commercial Road turnpike connecting the docks of East London with Barking. A new bridge was built in 1896, then in 1935 the present-day large steel bridge was built a little to the north and replaced the earlier bridge.

The 'Road to Empire', Silvertown, *c*. 1935. This aerial view of Silvertown Way shows the road shortly after completion. The building of this road was a major improvement as it eliminated long-standing traffic jams in Dockland caused by a series of level crossings and the need to keep opening road bridges over the dock basins to allow shipping in. The curving course of the Lea can be seen on the left, the Royal Victoria Dock on the right.

Silvertown bypass, *c*. 1935. The other component of interwar traffic improvements was the Silvertown bypass, a graceful concrete bow-string bridge which eased traffic flow between West Silvertown and Silvertown and thus between the Royal Victoria and Royal Albert Docks.

North Woolwich Road, *c.* 1884. Wagons trundle along the Silvertown Tramway, built in 1847 and serving for a time as the original rail route from Canning Town to North Woolwich. The Ram Tavern and Victoria Coffee and Dining Rooms stand on the far side. This area was the very heart of industrial West Ham with large factories stretching down to the Thames, particularly those from the chemical, brewing, sugar-making, and animal rendering industries.

West Marsh Sewer. A very bleak scene, but, behind the inquisitive boy posing on the sluice, houses are already springing up on the marshland. This view is somewhere near the present-day Manor Road. Much of the housing built on this low-lying land was jerry-built and erected without mains drainage, which led to persistent outbreaks of cholera and typhoid. The whole area had been the subject of a health investigation in 1855 led by Alfred Dickens, brother of the novelist.

Victoria Dock Road Level Crossing, *c*. 1903. A policeman stands guard at this notorious bottleneck, while behind, the vast bulk of the Black Prince rears over the wall of Thames Ironworks as the vessel nears completion. Thames Ironworks closed in 1910 after it was unable to compete with undercutting from Tyneside yards.

Tidal Basin Swing Bridge looking south, April 1904. This bridge was another black spot, partly because of its narrowness and partly because it was always being swung to allow shipping through.

Junction of Tidal Basin Road and Dock Road,
April 1904. An endless convoy of carts passes
the Clarendon Hotel on their way up to the
East India Dock Road, while a goods train roars
past on the Silvertown Tramway.

Channelsea River looking south from Abbey Mills, *c.* 1900. This dreary view belies the importance of the
Lea to industry; the river is seen here lined with barges. Industry, notably the manufacture of chemicals,
engineering and metalwork, clustered up against the Lea at Stratford, which indeed had its origins as an
industrial village.

TRANSPORT

*LTS Locomotive **Upton Park**. The London Tilbury & Southend Railway opened from Forest Gate to Tilbury in 1854 and two years later reached Southend, precipitating the growth of that seaside town. The distinctive LTS locomotives were originally all given names of places on the line's route, hence No. 6 was a 4-4-2 tank engine named Upton Park, built in 1880 and scrapped in 1932.*

Locomotive shop at Stratford Railway Works. Stratford was the site of the Great Eastern's main railway works from 1847. This 1891 photograph shows the erecting shop with a veritable production line of engines.

Carriage shop at Stratford Railway Works. Carriages are being widened from 4-seat pattern to 6-abreast. The works were closed in 1963.

Forest Gate station, *c.* 1905. Forest Gate first opened in 1840 as part of the Eastern Counties Railway. It became a junction station when the LTS Railway was opened for traffic on 13 April 1854.

Forest Gate station, *c.* 1903. The station was extensively rebuilt in 1870, the new station featuring a distinctive dome which has survived a further reconstruction in the 1990s.

Plaistow station, *c.* 1902. The LTS line to Southend originally ran via Tilbury but a direct line via Plaistow and East Ham was opened in 1858.

Looking towards Plaistow station, *c.* 1904. There was a small LTS railway works at Plaistow station between about 1876 and 1934.

Upton Park station, *c.* 1902. The station stands on the left-hand (West Ham) side of Green Street and was opened in 1877.

Canning Town station, 1933. First opened in 1846 as part of the North Woolwich branch of the Eastern Counties Railway, this station saw a vast daily traffic in workmen during the heyday of the Royal Docks. It is being revitalized in 1996 as a complex interchange is constructed connecting it with LTS, Docklands Light Railway and Jubilee lines.

Entrance to Stratford Railway Works, *c.* 1905. In this scene workmen pour out of the works into Great Eastern Street.

Inauguration of West Ham Tramways electric tram service. This grand ceremony took place on 27 February 1904.

West Ham corporation tram *en route* to Canning Town station. A posed, but still splendid, photograph — note the fine wrought iron gate at the rear and the driver's proud expression.

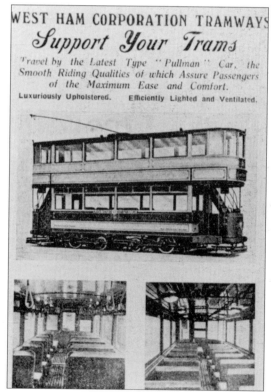

Advertisement for West Ham Corporation Tramways. Local authority tramways were the subject of considerable civic pride. This poster dates from 1928 and shows a fully enclosed tram, the last word in municipal transport in its day. In 1933 local tram services were taken over by the London Passenger Transport Board.

Accident at Stratford Bus Station. This unfortunate incident took place on the No. 86 route in Stratford
Bus Station in the 1970s!

Euston Arch. To round off this selection of transport photographs is the Euston Arch, a potent icon of the
railway age. The reason for its inclusion here is that after its demolition in 1967 the arch was dumped in
pieces into the Lea by Stratford to fill a deep riverbed hole. It lies there to this day and at the time of
writing ambitious plans have been announced to raise the remains and rebuild the arch.

WAR

Silvertown Fire Station after the Silvertown explosion. On 19 January 1917 50 tons of TNT blew up at the Brunner Mond chemical works, which had been converted to munitions production to help the war effort. Seventy-three people died and over 300 were injured in the blast, which was heard by the King at Sandringham and along the South Coast. At first rumours circulated that the factory had been bombed by a Zeppelin covered in invisible paint.

Distributing relief after the Silvertown explosion. The widespread destruction left hundreds homeless and local efforts were made to bring relief to the displaced residents. This picture shows members of the Barking Road Methodist Church ready to distribute food.

Peace tea, New Providence Street, Stratford, June 1919. The November 1918 armistice was greeted with riotous relief and, following the signing of the final peace in Versailles the following year, peace teas were organized across West Ham. Residents of New Providence Street pose in fancy dress in front of flags of the allied nations.

Peace tea, Ethel Road, Custom House, 19 July 1919. Another fancy dress peace tea, this time in the south of the borough.

Blitz damage, Silvertown Rubber Factory. The heavy industries concentrated along the Thames and the docks were repeatedly bombed during the Blitz, which lasted until November 1940.

Blitz damage, Cundy Road, Custom House. The date is Friday 6 September 1940, the day before the start of the Blitz proper on 'Black Saturday'.

War memorial at East London Cemetery. This rugged monument commemorates all the war dead of the British Empire killed in the First World War. There is also a mass grave of West Hammers killed in the Blitz with a monument to their sacrifice.

War blight, Plaistow, 1949. After the Second World War West Ham faced a massive task of reconstruction. Over a quarter of the borough's housing stock had been destroyed and the opportunity was taken to finish the job of slum clearance which the Luftwaffe had begun. This view shows waste ground – subsequently built over – looking from Balaam Street across to Grange Road, Plaistow.

ACKNOWLEDGEMENTS

I would like to thank all the members of Newham History Society, which in 1996 celebrated its Silver Jubilee, for all the encouragement received over the years.

I am grateful to the London Borough of Newham for permission to reproduce some of the images used in this volume.

Thanks are also due to Ken Langford, Crofton Osmotherley and Walter Scott for permission to use their photographs.

All other pictures are from the author's own postcard collection or reproduced by permission of the Eclipse Archive. Special thanks go to Lynn.

I also record my gratitude to my wife, Paulette, for all her technical assistance.